BUSINESS
SUCCESS

CHARLES M. SCHWAB

Business Success by Charles M. Schwab

ISBN 13 TP: 978-1-64095-329-1

CONTENTS

Introduction   5

Chapter 1   Thinking Beyond Your Job   15

Chapter 2   How Employees Are Appraised   27

Chapter 3   Seizing Your Opportunities   37

Chapter 4   The College Graduate in Business   45

Chapter 5   What Your Employer Expects   55

Chapter 6   My Twenty Thousand Partners   61

Chapter 7   People I Have Worked With   71

Chapter 8   On the Fundamental Elements
            of Success   79

Conclusion   91

INTRODUCTION

Anyone can rise to the heights of achievement if they dedicate themselves to personal and professional growth through hard work, ingenuity, and service to their fellow human beings. The proof for this statement is found in the life of Charles M. Schwab (1862–1939), an American businessman who was born into modest circumstances in Williamsburg, Pennsylvania, and amassed a large fortune as he advanced through various positions within the steel industry.

When Schwab was twelve, his parents moved to Loretto, a small town near Williamsburg. At the age of fifteen, he began assisting his father, a woolworker, with his contract to deliver mail by driving the wagon between

Loretto and Crescent, a neighboring town. An entrepreneur at an early age, Schwab would stop in the larger town of Cresson to meet travelers at the railroad station and assist them with their luggage. When he was seventeen, without finishing high school, he moved seventy miles away to Braddock, Pennsylvania, where he took a job at a grocery store that paid ten dollars a month plus room and board. During the day, he worked in the store as a clerk; after hours, he served as the night watchman. It was in Braddock that he developed a fascination for the steel works, where he would spend any free time he had.

As the story goes, one day Captain Bill Jones, the highly respected superintendent of Andrew Carnegie's Edgar Thomson Steel Works in Braddock, came into the grocery store where Schwab was working, and the young man asked Jones directly for a job.

Schwab was hired to drive spikes at the rate of a dollar a day, raising his monthly salary by fifteen dollars. Through his remarkable work ethic, he became chief of the engineering corps within six months. In fact, the story with which Schwab opens the first chapter of *Business Success* is about his first major promotion. Jones needed a supervisor for an important new engineering project, so he told the head of engineering to ask all the draftsmen to work late that evening without extra pay. Observing the young workers, Jones noticed that all of them were regularly checking the clock, with the exception of one—Schwab— who was completely absorbed in his work. Jones hired him to manage the project, and Schwab continued to grow his position, salary, and influence from that point on.

Schwab earned the respect of everyone with whom he worked for his enthusiasm about his job, friendly disposition, collaborative spirit, creativity, and economy. While at the Edgar Thomson Steel Works, he heightened the plant's efficiency and expanded the rail mill department until it had the highest production in the world, earning the praise of Carnegie himself.

In 1886, Schwab became the general superintendent of Homestead Steel Works, a plant Carnegie had recently acquired and was hoping to develop. His salary was set at ten thousand dollars a year—an impressive sum for a twenty-four-year-old. Under Schwab's direction, this facility innovated in new steelmaking processes to produce higher quality rails and, eventually, armor plate. To keep himself abreast of new developments in the chemistry of steel, Schwab built a lab in his home. Thanks to Schwab's efforts to improve the standard of armor, America became renowned for its well-built tanks and warships.

After a horrific furnace accident in 1889 killed Captain Jones, Schwab took over the Thomson Steel Works while also managing the Homestead Works. Eventually becoming general manager of Carnegie Steel, he inspired his employees through a bonus and profit-sharing system, settled union disputes, and worked alongside his laborers in both day and night shifts. In 1897, at only thirty-five years old, Carnegie offered him the position of president of Carnegie Steel. Schwab's salary was set at fifty thousand dollars, with an interest in the business.

On December 12, 1900, at a dinner of New York's elite businesspeople and bankers, Schwab delivered a speech in which he explained his vision for a massive steel organization that could guarantee low prices and job stability. The speech caught the attention of J. P. Morgan, who had recently financed the formation of General Electric. Morgan asked Schwab to list the companies that should be included in the industrial consolidation, and Schwab named Carnegie Steel. However, because he knew Carnegie would be hesitant about the deal, Schwab worked through Mrs. Carnegie, ultimately negotiating the sale of Carnegie Steel for four hundred million dollars of bonds for the new entity, the United States Steel Corporation. Schwab's interest in Carnegie Steel netted him roughly twenty-four million dollars, the equivalent today of about eight hundred million dollars. In the four years Schwab had been president of Carnegie Steel, he made approximately six million dollars a year, giving him the distinction of the highest salaried businessman in the world at the time.

When the US Steel Corporation was formed in 1901, Schwab served as its first president, but he left in 1903 to take over control of the Bethlehem Steel Company in Bethlehem, Pennsylvania. During his tenure at Bethlehem Steel, Schwab helped it become one of the largest steel producers in the world. Under his leadership, Bethlehem Steel pioneered the development of the H-beam, which transformed the construction industry and made the building of skyscrapers possible. When the Great Depression hit, Schwab's fortune was estimated to be between twenty-five and forty million dollars.

Schwab's formidable success can be attributed to his extraordinary work ethic, his ability to "think beyond the job," and his skill in motivating employees through profit sharing and harmonious workplace relations. In *Business Success*, he shares the principles that governed his personal and professional achievement—timeless maxims that will help any individual advance in their career and realize their vision of success. These principles are just as applicable today as they were when they were written. They dismantle the myths about success that are holding back countless individuals today. Primary among these is that you need natural talents, wealth, education, or genius to be successful. Not so, Schwab tells us. Hard work, enthusiasm, concentration, integrity, loyalty—these are the keys to greatness in life and in business.

Another myth that Schwab debunks is that you have to be ostentatious about your contributions to attract opportunities in your career. As Schwab tells us, "The people who attract attention are the ones who are thinking all the time and expressing themselves in little ways. It is not the ones who try to dazzle their employer by doing the theatrical, the spectacular." Perform your job with gusto, work smarter and better than your colleagues, do more than is expected, and think outside your specified role, and endless opportunity will be made available to you.

By applying the achievement principles in this book, you will enjoy the fruits of success that so few individuals experience—satisfaction with your circumstances, enjoyment of your work, and the overwhelming peace that comes from serving and developing others. Don't think that these concepts are meant for a select few; they are entirely democratic. As Schwab writes in a 1920 article, "Any man who goes into anything in life and does it better than the average will have a successful life."

A NOTE ON THE TEXT

The original manuscript has been slightly updated for modern application. When *Business Success* was first written, it was uncommon for women to advance in industry, so Schwab's audience was primarily men. Gendered language has been edited to expand the readership. In addition, the original chapter 8, "Woman's Part in Man's Success," has been removed to ensure maximum relevance in the modern world. We hope that regardless of your gender, location, education, etc., you will be inspired to improve your life and enlarge your pursuits. For as Schwab insists: "There's no limit possible to the expansion of each one of us."

CHAPTER ONE

THINKING BEYOND YOUR JOB

When old Captain Bill Jones, perhaps the greatest leader the steel business has ever known, was in control of the Braddock plant for Mr. Andrew Carnegie, a call came for an especially capable young individual to handle an important piece of engineering at Scotia.

Captain Bill knew people. He picked high-grade assistants with marvelous surety.

"Which one of your draftsmen shall we send up to Scotia?" he asked a superintendent.

"Why, any of them will fit the bill, Captain."

"But there must be one more capable than the others," commented Captain Bill. "Who is he?"

"I don't know," and the superintendent shook his head; "they are all bright, hustling youngsters."

Captain Bill stood in thought as his keen eyes ran down the red lines of furnaces. At last he said, "Tell every man to stick on the job until seven o'clock. I'll pick out Scotia's chief for you."

The order was a surprise. It was the slack season, when the draftsmen were not pressed to get through their work in regular hours. But they all kept on cheerfully.

As seven o'clock drew near, Captain Bill noticed that the men kept looking up to see how much more time they had to put in. All except one! Over in the corner, a young man was so absorbed that he seemed to have forgotten there was a clock in the room. When the hour finally came, the others hustled for their coats and hats. This chap was still bending over his desk. *He was the man whom Captain Bill sent up to Scotia.* One hardly needs to add that later he became the most valued engineer, a high-salaried man.

For thirty-six years, I have been moving among workers in what is now the biggest branch of American industry: the steel business. In that time, it has been my good fortune to watch most of the present leaders rise from the ranks, ascend step by step to places of power. These individuals, I am convinced, are not natural prodigies (endowed with extraordinary gifts or powers). *They won out by using normal brains to think beyond their daily duty.*

American industry is spilling over with individuals who started life even with the leaders, with brains just as big, with hands quite as capable. And yet one person emerges from the mass, rises sheer above their colleagues, and the rest remain.

The people who miss success have two general alibis: "I'm not a genius" is one; the other, "There aren't the opportunities today there used to be."

Neither excuse holds. The first is beside the point; the second is altogether wrong.

The thing that most people call "genius" I do not believe in. That is, I am sure that few successful individuals are so-called "natural geniuses."

The thing that most people call "genius" I do not believe in.

There is not a person in power at our Bethlehem steel works today who did not begin at the bottom and work their way up, round by round, simply by using their head and their hands a little more freely and a little more effectively than their co-workers. Eugene Grace, president of Bethlehem, worked in the yard when I first knew him. Mr. Snyder was a stenographer, Mr. Mathews a draftsman. The fifteen men in direct charge of the plants were selected not because of some startling stroke of genius but because, day in and day out, they were doing little unusual things—*thinking beyond their jobs.*

When I took over the Bethlehem works, I decided to train up its managers as Mr.

Carnegie trained his "boys." So I watched the workers who were already there and picked out a dozen. This selection took months. Then I set out to build an organization in which we should be bound together in harmony and kindly cooperation. I encouraged my managers to study iron and steel, markets and men. I gave them all small salaries but instituted a system whereby each person would share directly in the profits for which they were directly responsible. Every one of those individuals "came through." They are wealthy men today. All are directors of the company; some are directors of the corporation.

Most talk about "super-geniuses" is nonsense. I have found that when "stars" drop out, successors are usually at hand to fill their places; and the successors are merely individuals who have learned by application and self-discipline to get full production from an average, normal brain.

THINKING BEYOND YOUR JOB

Inventors, individuals with a unique, specialized talent, are the only real super-geniuses.
But they are so rare that they need no consider-
ation here.

I have always felt that the surest way to
qualify for the job just ahead is to work a
little harder than anyone else on the job one
is holding down. One of the most successful
people I have known never carried a watch
until he began to earn ten thousand dollars a
year. Before that, he had managed with a nickel
alarm clock in his bedroom, which he never
forgot to wind. Young men may enjoy dropping
their work at five or six o'clock and slipping
into a dress suit for an evening of pleasure, but
the habit has certain drawbacks. I happen to
know several able-bodied gentlemen who got
it so completely that now they are spending all
their time, days as well as evenings, in dress
suits, serving food in fashionable restaurants to

men who did not get the dress-suit habit until somewhat later in life.

> *The surest way to qualify for the job just ahead is to work a little harder than anyone else on the job one is holding down.*

Recently we have heard much about investments. To my mind, the best investment a young person starting out in business can possibly make is to give all their time, all their energies, to work—just plain, hard work. After an individual's position is assured, they can indulge in pleasure if they wish. They will have lost nothing by waiting—and gained much. They will have made money enough really to afford to spend some, and they will know that they have done right by themselves and by the world.

*The best investment a young person
starting out in business can possibly
make is to give all their time,
all their energies, to work—
just plain, hard work.*

The individuals who have done their best have done everything. Those who have done less than their best have done nothing.

Nothing is more fatal to success than taking one's job as a matter of course. If more people would get so enthused over their day's work that someone would have to remind them to get out to lunch, there would be more happiness in the world and less indigestion. If you must be a glutton, be a glutton for work. A trained ear can do tremendous business in the obstruction line. Sometimes it listens so intently for the toot of the quitting whistle that it quite loses the sense of spoken orders.

I have yet to hear an instance where misfortune hit a person because they worked overtime. I know lots of instances where it hit people who did not. Misfortune has many cloaks. Much more serious than physical injury is the slow, relentless blight that brings standstill, lack of advancement, final failure.

Those individuals who fail to give fair service during the hours for which they are paid are dishonest. Those who are not willing to give more than this are foolish.

In the modern business world, "pull" is losing its power. "Soft snaps" have been sponged off the slate. In most big companies, a thousand stockholders stand guard over the cashier's window, where formerly there were ten. The president's son starts at scratch. Achievement is the only test. The people who do the most are going to get the most pay, provided they show equal intelligence.

Captains of industry are not hunting for money. America is heavy in it. They are seeking brains—specialized brans—and faithful, loyal service. Brains are needed to carry out the plans of those who furnish the capital.

The people who attract attention are the ones who are thinking all the time and expressing themselves in little ways. It is not the ones who try to dazzle their employer by doing the theatrical, the spectacular. Those who attempt this are bound to fail.

CHAPTER TWO

HOW EMPLOYEES ARE APPRAISED

When I took charge of the Carnegie works at Homestead, there was a young chap employed there as water boy. A little later he became a clerk. I had a habit of going over the works at unusual hours to see how everything was moving. I noticed that no matter what time I came around, I would find the former water boy hard at work. I never learned when he slept.

Now, there seemed to be nothing remarkable about this fellow except his industry. The only way in which he attracted attention was by working longer hours and getting better results than anyone else. It was not long before we needed an assistant superintendent. The ex-water boy got the job. When we established our great armor plate department, there was not the slightest difference of opinion among the partners as to who should be manager. It was the youth with the inclination for overtime service.

Today that ex-water boy, Alva C. Dinkey, is head of a great steel company, and very wealthy. His rise was predicated on his willingness to work as long as there was any work to be done.

If a young person entering industry were to ask me for advice, I would say: Don't be afraid of giving a few extra hours to the company that pays your salary! Don't be reluctant about putting on overalls! Bare hands grip success better than kid gloves. Be thorough in all things, no matter how small or distasteful! The person who counts their hours and kicks about their salary is a self-elected failure.

It may be in seemingly unimportant things that a person expresses their passion for perfection, yet they will count heavily in the long run. When you go into your customary barber shop or salon, you will wait for the barber or stylist who gives you a little better haircut. Business leaders are looking for the same things in their offices that you look for in the barber shop or hair salon.

The real test of business greatness is in giving opportunity to others. Many businesspeople fail in this because they are thinking only of personal glory.

The real test of business greatness is in giving opportunity to others.

Several years ago, I was in conference with a New York banker when a newsboy entered the room to deliver a paper. After the boy had left, the banker said to me:

"For two years that boy has been bringing me papers every weekday. He comes exactly at the time I told him to come, three o'clock. He sells me a paper for just one cent and neither asks nor expects more. Now a boy who will attend to his business in that fashion has got the right kind of stuff in him. He doesn't know it yet, but I'm going to put him in my bank, and you may be sure he will be heard from."

Andrew Carnegie first attracted attention by using his head to think with. It was when he was a telegraph operator on the Pennsylvania Railroad under Colonel Thomas A. Scott. One morning a series of wrecks tangled up the line. Colonel Scott was absent, and young Carnegie could not locate him. Things looked bad.

Right then, Carnegie disregarded one of the road's strictest rules and sent out a dozen telegrams signed with Colonel Scott's name, giving orders that would clear the blockade.

"Young man," said the superintendent a few hours later, "do you realize that you have broken this company's rules?"

"Well, Mr. Scott, aren't your tracks clear and your trains running?" asked the young telegrapher.

Colonel Scott's punishment was to make Carnegie his private secretary. A few years later, when the colonel retired from office, he was succeeded by the former telegrapher, then only twenty-eight years old.

There is a young man in Bethlehem whom I expect to move up. This is the reason: Last winter there was an agitation at Washington which, if successful, would have smashed American shipping and wounded American business. We wanted to lay the matter before the President in its real significance. While we were pondering over ways to accomplish this, we got a message from the young man I have mentioned, saying he had seen the President, that the President understood the situation and had come to agree with us.

I wired for this young man to come on to Bethlehem. I wanted to see him. He had initiative; he had been thinking; he had arranged an interview with the President unprompted. In short, he was just the type of man that gladdens the heart of every employer.

> *People will succeed in anything about which they have real enthusiasm.*

Not long ago, a man was promoted in our works. "How did you happen to advance this fellow?" I asked his boss.

"Well," he explained, "I noticed that when the day shift went off duty and the night shift came on, this man stayed on the job until he had talked over the day's problems with his successor. That's why!"

I used to have a school friend in Philadelphia who had always impressed me as a forward-looking chap. So I was mightily surprised when he went into the manufacture of smoking pipes, his father's business. It seemed to me like a blind-alley choice.

To my surprise, this fellow made an astonishing success. When I met him, several years later, I asked how he had done it.

"Well," he said, "I found that ever so many people were making smoking pipes, all doing it in about the same way. If I wanted to make any dent, I had to do something different. I pondered ways and means. Finally, I decided that instead of having the stem run into the bottom of the bowl, I would raise it to the top, making it more sanitary, as well as novel. The idea caught on at once; it has made me hundreds of thousands of dollars. All I did was climb out of the rut into which other manufacturers had slumped."

People will succeed in anything about which they have real enthusiasm, in which they are genuinely interested, provided they will take more thought about their job than the individuals working with them. Those individuals who sit still and do only what they are told will never be told to do great things.

Those individuals who sit still and do only what they are told will never be told to do great things.

Jimmie Ward, one of our vice presidents, used to be a stenographer. But he kept doing things out of his regular line of duty. He reminded me of appointments and suggested little things that helped me get through my work. He was thinking beyond his job, so I gave him a better one. And he has gone up and up.

CHAPTER THREE

SEIZING YOUR OPPORTUNITIES

Eugene Grace is a striking example of what may be accomplished by the person with their eyes fixed beyond their pay envelope. Grace's ability to outthink his job, coupled with his sterling integrity, lifted him to the presidency of our corporation. Eight years ago, he was switching engines in the yards at Bethlehem. Last year, he earned more than a million dollars, and I predict that before long he will be perhaps the biggest man in industrial America.

Even in the humble job of switching engines, Grace made himself felt—there is no job too commonplace to express the individuality of an uncommon person. So he was put to operating an electric crane. Then he passed to the open hearth department, at fifteen dollars a week. I watched the fellow: I saw that he was seething with the stuff of which big men are built. He was not strong physically, but that body housed a dynamo of enthusiasm.

There is no job too commonplace to express the individuality of an uncommon person.

He was made yard foreman, then yard superintendent. When we wanted to reorganize the Juragua iron mines in Cuba, Grace got the job. His success was so solid that on his return, he was made assistant superintendent to the general manager who had charge of building the twenty-million-dollar Saucon plant at South Bethlehem. Soon he became general superintendent and, only a year later, general manager.

It is a pleasure to do business with Grace. His splendid enthusiasm goes hand in hand with absolute integrity. If he makes a statement, you can bet a million on it. You know he is right. This integrity has gone far toward winning him the position he holds today.

Integrity, incidentally, is one of the mightiest factors in salesmanship. If you have a reputation for stating facts exactly, for never attempting to gain momentary advantage through exaggeration, you possess the basis of all successful salesmanship.

Next to integrity comes personality—that indefinable charm that gives to people what perfume gives to flowers. Many of us think of salespeople as individuals traveling around with sample kits. Instead, we are all salespeople, every day of our lives. We are selling our ideas, our plans, our energies, our enthusiasm to those with whom we come in contact. Thus, the individual with a pleasing disposition is bound to accomplish much more, under similar conditions, than the person without it. If you have personality, cherish it; if you have not, cultivate it. For personality *can* be cultivated, although the task is not easy.

Nothing is so plentiful in America as opportunity. There are more jobs for dynamic individuals than there are dynamic individuals to fill them. Whenever the question comes up of buying new works, we never consider whether we can make the works pay. That is a foregone conclusion if we can get the right person to manage them.

*Nothing is so plentiful in America
as opportunity.*

All successful employers of labor are pursuing workers who will do the unusual, people who think, people who attract attention by performing more than is expected of them. These individuals have no difficulty in making their worth felt. They stand out above their colleagues until their superiors cannot fail to see them.

When A. D. Mixsell, one of our vice presidents, died a few months ago, everyone knew instinctively that his place would be taken by a man named Lewis, an assistant in the auditing department, making, perhaps, two hundred dollars a month. Both Mr. Grace and I picked him out before either had consulted the other. He simply stood out head and shoulders above everyone else.

It is a grave mistake to think that all the great American fortunes have been made; that all the country's resources have been developed. People make opportunity. Every great industrial achievement has been the result of individual effort—the practical development of a dream in the mind of an individual.

> *It is a grave mistake to think that all the great American fortunes have been made.*

I know a young New York fellow who has built himself a big business. He used to be a poorly paid clerk in a department store.

One rainy day, when customers were few, the clerks had gathered in a bunch to discuss baseball. A woman came into the store wet and disheveled. The baseball fans did not disband; but this young fellow stepped out of the circle and walked over to the woman. "What can I show you, madam?" he asked, smiling. She told him. He got the article promptly, laid it out before her, and explained its merits courteously and intelligently. In short, he treated the woman just as his employer would have treated her under similar circumstances. When the woman left, she asked for his card.

Later the firm received a letter from a woman ordering complete furnishings for a great estate in Scotland. "I want one of your men, Mr. _____," she wrote, "to supervise the furnishing personally." The name she mentioned was that of the clerk who had been courteous that rainy day.

"But, madam," said the head of the firm, a few days later, "this man is our youngest and most inexperienced clerk. Now, hadn't we better send Mr. _____?"

"I want this young man and no other," broke in the woman.

Large orders impose their own conditions. So our courteous young clerk was sent across the Atlantic to direct the furnishing of a great Scottish palace.

His customer that rainy day had been Mrs. Andrew Carnegie.

The estate was Skibo Castle.

CHAPTER FOUR

THE COLLEGE GRADUATE IN BUSINESS

The relation of higher education to industry always has interested me. Several years ago, I spoke to a little group of New York boys from the East Side on the subject of business success. These youngsters were spending their evenings in hard study after working all day for a living, a splendid indication that they had the right stuff in them.

I told these boys that if they kept to their course, they stood as good a chance of success as anyone in the world—a better chance, in fact, than many young people entering college at their age instead of stepping out into the world of practical affairs. "The higher education for which these young individuals were giving up three or four of their best years," I said, "holds no advantage of itself in the coming business battle. It will be valueless industrially unless it is accompanied by a capacity for plain, hard work; for concentration; for clear thinking. These qualities are not learned in textbooks."

> *Higher education holds no advantage of itself. It will be valueless unless it is accompanied by a capacity for plain, hard work; for concentration; for clear thinking.*

To my utter surprise, the newspapers the next day quoted me as being opposed to a college education, indeed, to education in any form. They declared that I despised learning and believed the time spent in getting it was wasted. This false impression has had a long life. Even today it crops up occasionally.

I am not against a college education. I never have been. Whatever may have been true in the past, there is no doubt that today industrial conditions favor the college graduate. Old crudities are disappearing; science is dethroning chance. Business is conducted on so vast a scale that the broadening effects of higher education, gained through proper application, write a large figure.

But the college graduate who thinks that their greater learning gives them the privilege of working less hard than those without such an education is going to wake up in disaster. I regret that some college graduates enter industry with an inflated notion of their own value. They want to capitalize at once on their education and the time they spent getting it. They feel it is unfair to begin at the bottom, on the same basis with a youth of seventeen or eighteen who has never been to college.

A college graduate, entering industry, is worth no more to their employer than a secondary school or high school graduate, unless they happen to be taking up some position in which higher education is directly applied. Even then, they have to make adjustments. Neither knowledge of the classics nor mathematical proficiency can be converted overnight into a marketable commodity.

Higher education has its chance later, when the college graduate has mastered all the minor details of the business. Then, if they went to college with serious purpose and studied hard and systematically, they have the advantage of a thoroughly trained mind to tackle larger problems, a mind which should be broader and more flexible because of its greater powers of imagination and logical reasoning.

Real success is won only by hard, honest, persistent toil. Unless a young person gets accustomed to that in school, they are going to have a very hard time getting accustomed to it outside. The person who goes to college only because it suits their parents to send them and who drifts dreamily through their classes gets a disagreeable jolt when they land a job outside with a salary attached to it.

Furthermore, if the college graduate thinks that their education gives them a higher social status, they are riding for a fall. Some college graduate, too—not the average ones, fortunately—have a pride in their mental attainments that is almost arrogance. Employers find it difficult to control, guide, and train such individuals. Their spirit of superiority bars the path of progress.

> *A spirit of superiority bars the path of progress.*

Most college graduates are free from this false pride. But occasionally employers come in contact with someone who has it and judge all college graduates by them. In business, we buy samples, and sometimes the wrong sort of sample from an institution of higher learning makes an employer feel as Robert Hall felt when he wrote of Kippis that "He might be a very clever man by nature, for aught I know, but he laid so many books on top of his head that his brains could not move."

While I have no sympathy with this occasional prejudice against college graduates, yet I have found frequently that the very fact of having been denied a higher education works in favor of the common schoolboy or girl. They have to labor after hours for their education; nights and holidays they have hammered at the forge of ambition. College graduates are likely to think their evenings are meant for music, society, good times, rather than for study that will add to their business knowledge.

For some college graduates it is a hard descent from the heights of theory to the plains of everyday facts and common sense. Sometimes years of book learning come to grief before a problem that is disposed of out of hand by individuals whose wits have been sharpened to an edge by practical, everyday experience.

Thomas A. Edison, who never saw the inside of a college as a student, once had in his laboratory a man fresh from one of our great universities, where he had graduated at the head of his class. Soon this young Bachelor of Arts met much that upset his pet theories. When things were done contrary to rules laid down in the books, he looked on with indulgence.

One day, Mr. Edison unscrewed from its socket an incandescent electric light bulb. "Find the cubic contents of this!" he said to the college graduate.

To work out the problem by mathematical procedure was about as difficult as squaring the circle. But the college student went at it boldly. Reams of paper were figured and disfigured by his energetic pencil during the next few days. Finally, he brought to Mr. Edison the result of his calculations. "You're at least ten percent out of the way," said the inventor. The graduate, sublimely confident, disputed this.

"All right," said Edison calmly. "Let's find out."

The graduate took out his pencil, ready for another encounter with mathematics; but the inventor quietly picked up a small hammer and knocked the tip off the blown end of the bulb. Then he filled the bulb with water, weighed it, and in about a minute had arrived absolutely at the result. It showed that the complex mathematical calculations of the college graduate were at least ten percent off.

Fortunately, the lesson went home, and afterward the star student became an excellent practical electrician.

CHAPTER FIVE

WHAT YOUR EMPLOYER EXPECTS

Bethlehem's biggest asset is not its rolling mill plants, its gun shops, its armor works, its rail mills; it is the individuals who make up its enthusiastic organization. For more than thirty years I have been superintending the manufacture of steel, and I can say that my employees at Bethlehem are the most energetic, competent, and lovable people with whom I have ever worked.

To no small extent, the success of Bethlehem has been built up by our profit-sharing system. But coupled with this individual incentive to extra effort is a corps loyalty, a friendly rivalry, without which no great business can reach the maximum of production.

I love to appeal to the American spirit of conquest in my employees, the spirit of doing things better than anyone has ever done them before. There is nothing to which individuals respond more quickly.

Once when I was with Mr. Carnegie, I had a mill manager who was finely educated, thoroughly capable, and master of every detail of the business. But he seemed unable to inspire his workers to do their best.

"How is it that a man as able as you," I asked him one day, "cannot make this mill turn out what it should?"

"I don't know," he replied. "I have coaxed the men; I have pushed them; I have sworn at them. I have done everything in my power. Yet they will not produce."

All individuals should get exactly what they make themselves worth.

It was near the end of day; in a few minutes, the night force would come on duty. I turned to a workman who was standing beside one of the red-mouthed furnaces and asked him for a piece of chalk.

"How many heats has your shift made today?" I queried.

"Six," he replied.

I chalked a big "6" on the floor and then passed along without another word. When the night shift came in, they saw the "6" and asked about it.

"The big boss was in here today," said the day men. "He asked us how many heats we had made, and we told him six. He chalked it down."

The next morning, I passed through the same mill. I saw that the "6" had been rubbed out and a big "7" written instead. The night shift had announced itself. That night I went back. The "7" had been erased and a "10" written in its place. The day force recognized no superiors. Thus a fine competition was started, and it went on until this mill, formerly the poorest producer, was turning out more than any other mill in the plant.

The Bethlehem profit-sharing system is based on my belief that all individuals should get exactly what they make themselves worth. This is the only plan I know of which is equally fair to the employers and every class of employee. Someday, I hope, all labor troubles will be solved by such a system.

CHAPTER SIX

MY TWENTY THOUSAND PARTNERS

I am not a believer in large salaries. I hold that every individual should be paid for personal production. Our executives at Bethlehem seldom get salaries of over one hundred dollars a week; but all of them receive bonuses—computed entirely on the efficiencies and the economies registered in their departments.

Approximately eighty percent of the twenty-two thousand employees in our plants at Bethlehem come under the operation of the system. The only ones not included are certain kinds of day laborers, whose work is of such a nature that it does not fall readily into the scheme, and the workers in a few special or too-complex departments.

Every individual should be paid for personal production.

Take the case of a mechanic: he is given a certain piece of work, and he knows that the allotted time for doing this work is, say, twenty hours. Perhaps he has a regular wage of forty cents an hour, irrespective of his production. If he finishes the job in the allotted twenty hours, he gets a bonus of twenty percent, bringing his total pay for the work up to nine dollars and sixty cents, and is ready forthwith to tackle another piece of work. In other words, the man gets bonus pay for the job on the basis of the *entire schedule time*, regardless of the actual time it takes him to do it.

Any shortcuts an employee may devise or any unusual energy they may show are thus capitalized into profit for them. With this stimulus, our employees are always giving their best efforts to their work, and the result has been that the production per employee in some departments has more than doubled since the plan was put into effect.

We have complete schedules of time and bonus rates for many kinds of common labor, and our statistics show that such labor has been averaging nearly forty percent above the regular rate per hour. Such jobs as wheeling a wheelbarrow or handling a shovel have been put under the profit-sharing system.

There are some departments in which the work is of such a nature that time enters very slightly into calculation—in open hearth work or the treating of armor plate, for example.

Here we are more concerned with the *quality* of the work than with the quantity turned out in a given time. In these cases, we give a bonus for quality, basing our computations on tests of the steel. If we had the regular system in operation here, employees might be tempted to hurry their work, and a lot of steel would have to be thrown out.

In still other departments we give bonuses for efficiencies. If an employee handles their machines so that the item or repair is very low, or if they get equal results with less than the regular amount of fuel, they are paid accordingly. We try to take into calculation every element that depends on the initiative, or originality, or energy, or manual dexterity of a worker.

In many departments, we use $1 as a unit cost standard. The manager or superintendent gets 1 percent of the reduction down to $0.95, 2 percent of the total from $0.95 to $0.90, 3 percent of the total from $0.90 to $0.85, and so on. This holds out every inducement for economy and efficiency.

We say to the superintendent of blast furnaces, for example: "This is your normal operation cost, the amount we charge up. Everything you save from this standard cost you will share; and the more money you make, the more money we will make, and the more satisfied everybody will be."

If Mr. Grace, the president of Bethlehem, who made a million dollars last year, were working on a salary, he would have been very well paid if he had got thirty or forty thousand dollars. But I am delighted to see him make a million. If he had made two million, the corporation would have made that much more.

We have to have a very elaborate and very costly statistical department to carry out the system, but it pays for itself a hundred times over.

There is at Bethlehem a minimum wage below which no employee's salary shall fall. But most of what each worker earns is made up of bonuses. We find that if an employee has not ambition enough to earn bonuses, they are not likely to remain with us long.

I am very happy to know that my Bethlehem employees are the best paid body of workers in the steel industry in America. Last year, from superintendents to entry-level workers, they averaged $990 apiece.

Systems of general profit sharing have certain disadvantages from which ours is free.

One disadvantage is that the lazy employee shares the reward of the smart employee's work. General systems give employees uniformly bigger wages in times of general prosperity and furnish a good excuse to reduce wages at other times.

My system, I believe, can be fitted to any branch of industry. A banker once told me that there was no way in which it could be worked out for banks. I told him I thought there was a way. And to prove it I devised a system which has been put into successful operation in a dozen banks.

Profit sharing works well almost anywhere. I use it in my own home. Not long ago, the expenses of running my New York house got exorbitant. I called in the steward and said to him:

"George, I want to strike a bargain with you. I will give you ten percent of the first thousand dollars you save in house expenses, twenty-five percent of the second thousand, and one-half of the third thousand."

The expense of operating the house was cut in two.

> *You cannot make employees think you are interested in them unless you really are.*

Individuals are pretty keen judges of their employers. You cannot make employees think you are interested in them unless you really are. They realize at once whether your interest is real or feigned.

The leader who gets the loyalty of his employees is the person who has, first of all, a reputation for fair dealing. Employees gauge fair dealing quickly and respond to it.

There has never been so much solidarity in business, so close a spirit of cooperation between employers and workers, as there is today. It is time for Americans to realize the falseness of the cry that we are a nation of money-grabbers. The difference between us and other nations is that we know how to earn money, while they, in the main, know how to save it. The sordid, hoarding miser, who makes every sacrifice to accumulate, is so scarce with us as to cut no figure, while abroad he is everywhere.

CHAPTER SEVEN

PEOPLE I HAVE WORKED WITH

Whenever problems of managing people come to my mind, I think of my old master, Captain W. R. Jones, the man who, Henry Bessemer said, knew more about steel than any other man in America.

Old Captain Bill started in at Johnstown as a monkey-wrench mechanic back in 1874 or 1875 and then went with Mr. Carnegie to Braddock—Mr. Carnegie's first steel venture. He was manager of the Braddock works when I entered the steel business under him in 1880, and I have never felt a deeper and more lasting affection for any man than I had for old Captain Bill.

Uneducated, unpolished, outspoken, old Captain Bill was one of the most magnificent leaders of men America has ever produced. Everybody who worked for him idolized him, and this idolatry made it possible for him to break all previous records in steel production.

Captain Bill could never understand the chemistry of the steel business, which was just then beginning to reform the old hit-or-miss program. I remember very well the first time the Pennsylvania Railroad specified that the rails we furnished should be of a certain chemical composition. This alarmed the old captain. He had never heard such names as carbon and manganese.

"Charlie," he said to me one day, "this damn chemistry is going to ruin the steel business yet."

In those days, of course, the steel business was in its infancy. Our expansion since then has surpassed belief. In 1880, the whole country produced less than a million tons of steel. In 1890, the amount had risen to five million tons; in 1900, about thirteen million; in 1910, over twenty million; and this year we shall produce over forty million tons of steel in America.

Once I wrote to Mr. Carnegie about a rail mill which we had designed at Braddock and announced enthusiastically that when the mill was completed, it would roll over a thousand tons of rails a day.

"I see no objection to the amount of money you want to spend," Mr. Carnegie wrote back, "but I want to exact one promise from you, that you will never tell anyone we were foolish enough to suppose that this country would ever require a mill to make one thousand tons of rails a day."

Now, think of us, after this short time, making from twelve thousand to fifteen thousand tons of steel rails a day!

In 1886, it fell to my lot to roll the first steel girder that ever went into a skyscraper. At that time, the business promised little. But today more than five million tons of steel are used annually for buildings. In 1901, I built the first steel railway car; now more than five million tons of steel a year are used for that purpose.

Old Captain Bill Jones was a man of many original notions. For instance, he would never take the partnership that Mr. Carnegie offered him repeatedly. He said he didn't want the men to think he was sharing the profits of the company. After trying in vain to change his manager's mind, Mr. Carnegie declared that he would always pay Captain Bill as much as the President of the United States was getting. And he always did.

The captain, I remember, used to characterize Mr. Carnegie as a wasp that came buzzing around to stir up everybody. One hot day in early summer, Mr. Carnegie sought out Jones in the works.

"Captain," he said, "I'm awfully sorry to leave you in the midst of hot metals here, but I must go to Europe. I can't stand the sultry summer of this country. You have no idea, Captain, when I get on the ship and get out of sight of land, what a relief it is to me."

"No, Andy," flashed the captain, "and you have no idea what a relief it is to me, either."

On one occasion I was talking with Hebert Spencer, Mr. Gladstone, and Mr. Carnegie in England. Each of us was supposed to contribute something entertaining to the conversation, and for a while I was rather puzzled to know what to say that would interest these famous men. Finally, I decided I would tell them some stories about the old captain, and I told them many. One of the things I prize most is a letter from Mr. Spencer recalling those stories.

> *Kindness to everybody always*
> *pays for itself.*

Mr. Carnegie was the first big American businessman to inaugurate a real profit-sharing system. He was the epitomization of unselfishness. Perhaps the way in which Mr. Carnegie differed from many employers could be illustrated by calling up the picture of two boys about to feast. One says: "I have a nice pie. Come, let's eat it."

Mr. Carnegie's personality would enthuse anybody who worked for him. He had the broad views of a really big man. He was not bothered with the finicky little things that trouble so many people. When he made me manager, Mr. Carnegie said: "Now, boy, you will see a good many things which you mustn't notice. Don't blame your men for trivial faults. If you do, you will dishearten them."

When I want to find fault with my men, I say nothing when I go through their departments. If I were satisfied, I would praise them. My silence hurts them more than anything else in the world, and it doesn't give offense. It makes them think and work harder.

Many leaders fail because they do not see the importance of being kind and courteous to the workers under them. Kindness to everybody always pays for itself. And, besides, it is a pleasure to be kind. I have seen people lose important positions, or their reputations—which are more important than any position—by little careless discourtesies to those whom they did not think it was worthwhile to be kind to.

CHAPTER EIGHT

ON THE FUNDAMENTAL ELEMENTS OF SUCCESS

My success is due to the fact that in the first place, I stood on my own feet—always relied on myself. It is really a detriment to have anyone behind you. When you depend on yourself, you know that it is only on your own merit that you succeed. Then you discover your latent powers, awaken to your potential, and are motivated to do your uttermost. It is a very good motto to depend on yourself. I am a great believer in self-reliant individuality.

No one ever made a success of their life by luck, or chance, or accident. When you come across one of that vast majority who have failed because they "never had a chance," you'll take notice that they lack that indefinable, subtle something that stands for success; and sometimes I'm inclined to believe the mysterious something is simply a capacity and a disposition for hard work.

I am a great believer in self-reliant individuality.

The rich man's child enters life's race with a handicap. Not only the handicap which a fortune is, because it deprives them of the necessity to progress and expand, but the handicap of never being able to appreciate what they've got. For everything in life that's worthwhile is ten times more worthwhile when we yearn and work and climb for it.

The first great blessing in my life was being born poor. The fundamental principles that founded my character were the lessons wrung out of early hardships, and privations, and self-denials. I would not give up the experience of a boyhood barren of luxuries and paved with obstacles for any amount of money. It would be like pulling the foundation out of a building.

At an age when boys of today are petted and pampered, I learned the size and value of a dollar. I learned all that it stood for in comforts and in working principle, and I learned all the labor it stood for. And incidentally, I realized that every one of those dollars that figured in my life would mean just so much honest labor on my part.

The first great blessing in my life was being born poor.

Fortunately, I realized, too, that the plan worked both ways; that every dollar's worth of work I executed would be paid for in coin of the realm, whether it was overtime, whether it was bargained for, whether it came out of this employer's pocket or the next one, or, indeed, whether the present employer knew of it at all.

Some employer, I knew, would pay me full value for every hour's work I put in, for I was stowing away, as a stock in trade, every moment's work and its subsequent knowledge and experience. I am a hearty believer in the law of compensation. I don't believe an honest effort ever goes unrewarded, though sometimes the reward is a long time coming.

There are many reasons why people are always working and not always succeeding. Sometimes they belong to the class who cultivate the appearance of working, doing anything. Sometimes they spend their lives working, bemoaning the fact that it's all effort and no reward, and lay down the scythe just before the harvest ripens.

Hope and faith and courage are just as essential to success as the necessary effort. Many an individual has lain down just this side of their laurels and neither they nor the world ever knew how near they came to accomplishment.

Then there are people who work conscientiously, perseveringly, hopefully; but they're working on the wrong course of action. I believe that such individuals realize they're out of place and out of tune and will never strike the harmonious chord that accomplishment is. But they resolve they've got a little start and don't want to lose it. These people form part of the army that fails.

I do not believe there is a person living who has not a capacity for some one line of work, who could not excel in that line if they pursued it.

I do not believe there is a person living who has not a capacity for some one line of work, who could not excel in that line if they pursued it. The first essential in a person's career is to find out what they are fitted for, what they're most capable of doing and doing with enthusiasm.

The second essential is to go to work and do it, no matter the cost, no matter the obstacles, no matter the sacrifices. And if a person is going to stand out among the others, they've got to resolve to do the particular thing they've fastened on better than anyone else.

Everyone's got it in them, if they'll only make up their mind and stick at it. None of us is born with a stop-valve on our powers or with a set limit to our capacities. There's no limit possible to the expansion of each one of us.

It all depends upon our will and the power of our resolution. Our capacities expand and enlarge with exercise, just as the muscles of our bodies enlarge and grow strong.

That's the way character is formed—doing calisthenic feats with obstacles and adversities. I tell you, the hard knocks are the nest eggs of our fortunes. The people who are not made of the right stuff go under with them and are never heard of again.

There's no limit possible to the expansion of each one of us.

And there are others who are soured and embittered by them, and they're heard from eternally. They haven't a good word to say for the world's plan, because when it got a trifle complicated it baffled them.

Those are the people who do more harm to the youth of civilization than its vices. Then there are those who start out, sometimes with bare feet and holes in their clothes, bravely resolving never to let circumstances crush them, never to harbor bitterness over defeat, but to save their energies for the next encounter.

These are the individuals hard knocks don't hurt. They toughen them; they help them get ready for the next encounter. To these people, it's only a question of sufficient hardship, and sacrifice, and battle, to make them proof against any onslaught. These are the soldiers, the victors.

Did you ever find a successful soldier who hadn't seen a fight? That's why I say the rich man's child is born with a handicap, and it's why I think the man with a million and a child should keep the two a long way apart.

Heaven forbid that money should be the only thing to strive for. Beyond a certain point of requirement, money is useless to the individual. A vast fortune cannot do its full duty in the life of one person who inherits or makes it; it is destined to better the lives of hundreds.

The individuals who reap success are not those who aim to accumulate millions; they are the people who aim to do one thing, to do it better than anyone else can do it, to take it up from the very beginning and push it through to the end.

What satisfaction can there be in piling up vast wealth for the sake of wealth itself? The only part that money plays in success is as a reward. Money is the standard of value. It is the equivalent of merit. Money is the only coin in which we can pay for hard work or for genius, and so it is the equivalent of accomplishment.

But the individuals who reap success are not those who aim to accumulate millions; they are the people who aim to do one thing, to do it better than anyone else can do it, to take it up from the very beginning and push it through to the end. That is what makes success, and success means money.

For my own part, I am more interested in my work than its mere money value. Millions of dollars can never give me the pleasure I found in learning the intricate workings of a steel plant. Hitting upon a new device which, when applied to a machine with my own fingers, had a desired effect upon its workings, gave me the keenest possible satisfaction.

CONCLUSION

Now that you have read Schwab's success manifesto, it's time to implement the principles to advance your career. The stories in this book prove that success is democratic—anyone can progress in their organization and industry if they practice these time-tested strategies. The core elements of Schwab's success system are listed below for the benefit of your continued study and application.

"The only part that money plays in success is as a reward."

Don't think of earning wealth just for the sake of amassing a fortune. Money might be the reward for high achievement, but it should not be your primary motivation. Success comes to those who are driven by a desire to accomplish a major goal and who commit to seeing it through from start to finish.

"People will succeed in anything about which they have real enthusiasm."

Find reasons to be enthusiastic about your work. Absorb yourself in it so that while you are at work, you are not watching the clock, counting down the minutes until quitting time; and while you are at home, you are looking for ways to grow your understanding of your field. Enthusiasm yields knowledge, gains the trust and respect of colleagues and supervisors, and promotes personal joy. What's more, enthusiasm feeds into other crucial success traits, such as integrity and personality.

"There is no job too commonplace to express the individuality of an uncommon person."

As Schwab recommends, "Think beyond the job" or "Outthink your job." Find ways to improve the processes for which you are currently responsible. Seek out opportunities to add value to your organization. Do not be aggressive or showy in your innovations; rather, use the insight you gain to improve the efficiency and quality of your own work, and propose larger initiatives when the timing is right.

"Those individuals who sit still and do only what they are told will never be told to do great things."

In other words, go above and beyond in your daily responsibilities. Do not wait to be asked to do something; seek out opportunities for serving your department, organization, etc. Leaders will take notice of your initiative and dedication and reward you for it accordingly.

"The real test of business greatness is in giving opportunity to others."

Seek first to develop those with whom you work and to serve your greater community, and success will come to you, for it tends to pass over those who think primarily of personal glory. Schwab refused high-paying positions offered to him because they would not allow him to reward his employees in the manner he preferred. Because of his commitment to developing and rewarding his people, Schwab was a better worker and a better leader, which his positions (and accompanying salaries) reflected.

These principles form the backbone of a success program that is sure to help you reach and exceed your personal and professional goals. Reflect on them, study them individually and with the support of a mastermind group or book club, and, most importantly, put them into action. The earlier you begin performing at the higher level described by Schwab in this book, the sooner you will be able to realize *business success.*

Made in the USA
Middletown, DE
23 October 2023

41277606R00057